ESTHER'S BEST

RECIPE BOOK

ESTHER BRUNNING

Photography by Lucy Johnston

TWO TOWERS PRESS

For Richard, with much love xx

Text © Esther Brunning, 2012
Photography © Lucy Johnston, 2011
Photography & illustration © Kath Lees, 2012

First published in Great Britain in 2012 by
Two Towers Press, 2 High Street, Mistley, Essex, CO11 1HA
Reprinted in 2017
2 3 4 5 6 7 8 9

Design by Kath Lees
Typeset in Century Schoolbook & Franklin Gothic

British Library Cataloguing in Publication Data.
A catalogue record for this book is available from the British Library.

ISBN: 978–0–9573219–0–8

www.esthersbest.com

SIMPLY PERFECT RECIPES

ESTHER'S BEST
BEST
RECIPE BOOK

ZEST UP YOUR EVERYDAY COOKING

ESTHER BRUNNING
Photography by
Lucy Johnston

CONTENTS

ESTHER'S BEST RECIPE BOOK is the culmination of eight full years' of cooking on a daily basis for our many thousands of customers at the Mistley Quay Café in East Anglia. Many customers have become good friends, and have urged us to put together a book about what we've learned. So finally, here it is.

My own road to the Mistley Quay Café started at home with my Mum, and later at Leith's. After several years catering in central London I met Rich, and together we fell in love with the idea of starting a small business in Mistley, on the River Stour in Essex. We laid down our roots, got married, bought a house, started a family and the Café, all in the space of just a few years!

Our *oeuvre* has evolved in three main ways. Firstly, perhaps reflecting the usually sunny, dry climate in Mistley, my cooking has developed a Mediterranean flavour, often using spices, fruits and other exotic ingredients. Our travels to Turkey and Morocco have definitely left a preference for zingy flavours on my taste buds; and these flavours are one of the things our customers at the Café love too.

Secondly, good food for me means fresh ingredients and simple recipes. We always insist on using fresh, locally grown ingredients whenever possible (hence the book's design which makes reference to fresh produce packed and delivered in wooden boxes).

Thirdly, we are well-known across the region for our generous servings; we believe it's the healthy way to eat, discouraging snacking between meals. We hope this book encourages the same philosophy.

My biggest wish for *Esther's Best Recipe Book* is that it will help and inspire busy people with their everyday cooking. In my mind there's nothing better than enjoying good home-cooked food with family or friends, any day of the week, and I believe these recipes will help you do that with the minimum of effort.

One last note: gluten-free cooking has become an important, if not exclusive, part of the offering at our Café so I have highlighted the gluten-free recipes.

So, please enjoy the very best of my recipes; here they are in this book, simple, perfect and just a few steps away from zesting up your everyday cooking!

Esther

SOUPS

BROCCOLI AND STILTON SOUP
CARROT, SWEET POTATO AND GINGER SOUP
COURGETTE, TOMATO AND CANNELLINI BEAN SOUP
PEA AND MINT SOUP
SPINACH AND PUY LENTIL SOUP
TOMATO AND BASIL SOUP

BROCCOLI AND STILTON SOUP ⓖⓕ

Serves 4-6

2 tbsp olive oil

500g broccoli, cut into
  medium sized florets

300g potatoes, peeled and
  cut into chunks

2 onions, chopped

2 cloves garlic, crushed

1 litre Marigold bouillon

200g stilton, crumbled

100ml single cream

Salt and pepper

Chives, chopped

A DELICIOUS AND VERY EASY winter soup, serve with warm crusty bread and you can't go wrong!

—

Heat the oil in a large saucepan over a moderate heat. Add the onions and garlic, cook until soft and translucent. Add the potatoes and stock, bring to the boil. Reduce the heat and cook for about 15-20 minutes on a gentle simmer until the potatoes are soft.

Then add the broccoli for the last 5 minutes of cooking time. Stir in the stilton and cream. Allow to cool, put the soup in a food processor or liquidize with a hand blender.

Season with salt and freshly ground pepper. Serve hot with chives sprinkled on the top, and a swirl of cream.

CARROT, SWEET POTATO AND GINGER SOUP (GF)

Serves 4-6

2 tbsp olive oil

2 onions, chopped

500g carrots, peeled and
 chopped

2 sweet potatoes, peeled
 and chopped

1 garlic clove, crushed

3cm piece of fresh ginger,
 roughly chopped

3 celery sticks, chopped

1 red chilli or 1 tsp dried chilli
 (optional)

1 litre Marigold bouillon

Salt and pepper

Handful fresh coriander,
 chopped

A WARMING and very popular winter soup. More spices can be added depending on your palate.

—

Heat the oil in a large saucepan over a low heat. Add the onions, garlic, ginger and chilli if using. Cover the pan and cook until soft.

Add the carrots, sweet potatoes and celery. Pour over the hot stock, season and simmer for about 20 minutes - the test is that you should easily be able to crush a piece of carrot against the side of the pan with a wooden spoon.

Allow to cool, put the soup in a food processor or liquidize with a hand blender. Return to the pan, season to taste and thin the soup with more water if needed.

Serve with a sprinkling of chopped coriander and a swirl of cream.

COURGETTE, TOMATO AND CANNELLINI BEAN SOUP

Serves 4-6

2 tbsp olive oil

500g courgettes, cut into
  small chunks

1 tin chopped tomatoes

1 tin cannellini beans

2 onions, chopped

2 cloves garlic, crushed

4 fresh tomatoes, chopped
  roughly

1 litre Marigold bouillon

1 tbsp mixed herbs

Handful fresh basil, chopped

Salt and pepper

THIS IS A FUN SOUP, and as a friend said, very useful, as most children will love it. It also takes about 5 minutes to prepare and 10 to cook! Keep some cannellini beans in the store cupboard and when you have a spare couple of courgettes you can make this soup for a filling lunch.

—

Heat the oil in a large saucepan over a moderate heat. Add the onions and garlic, cook until soft and translucent. Then add the courgettes and cook for 3-4 minutes. Add the tinned tomatoes, mixed herbs and stock, bring to the boil. Reduce the heat and cook for about 5-10 minutes on a gentle simmer. Add fresh chopped tomatoes and cannellini beans, mix through and cook for further 3-4 minutes.

Allow to cool, add fresh basil, put soup in a food processor or liquidize with a hand blender. It is best with some texture left in so it's a good idea to liquidize half and leave the other half chunky.

Season with salt and freshly ground pepper.

PEA AND MINT SOUP ⒼⒻ

Serves 4-6

2 tbsp olive oil

2 onions, chopped

500g frozen or fresh peas,
  reserve 50g for decoration

2 medium potatoes, peeled
  and chopped

3 cloves garlic, crushed

1 litre Marigold bouillon

Handful fresh mint, chopped

Salt and pepper

THIS SOUP IS VERY TASTY eaten warm but it is equally delicious chilled in the summer when you feel like something cool and refreshing for lunch.

—

Heat the oil in a large saucepan over a moderate heat. Add the onions, potato and garlic. Cook for about 5 minutes. Add the hot stock, bring to the boil and simmer slowly for 10-15 minutes until the potatoes are soft.

When soft add the peas and cook for a further couple of minutes.

Cool for 5 minutes. Put the soup with the fresh mint in a food processor or liquidize with a hand blender. Return the pan to the heat and add the remaining peas.

Make sure the peas are cooked before serving warm with a swirl of cream if desired and a little fresh mint on top.

Season with salt and freshly ground pepper.

SPINACH AND PUY LENTIL SOUP ⒼⒻ

Serves 4-6

2 tbsp olive oil

500g spinach, frozen or fresh

200g puy lentils, rinsed

2 onions, chopped

2 cloves garlic, crushed

1 litre Marigold bouillon

1 tsp nutmeg

Salt and pepper

Chives, chopped

JUST RECENTLY made this soup up as it was a cold and miserable January day. Wow! It was good, it warmed us all up and felt very virtuous to eat; practically zero fat which certainly appealed!

———

Heat the oil in a large saucepan over a moderate heat. Add the onions and garlic, cook until soft and translucent. Add the puy lentils and cook for about 25 minutes on a gentle simmer until soft. Then add the spinach until cooked. Allow to cool, put the soup in a food processor or liquidize with a hand blender.

As the lentils are thick you may need to water it down before serving. Leave some unliquidized if you like a soup with some texture to it.

Season with salt and freshly ground pepper.

TOMATO AND BASIL SOUP ⓖ

Serves 4-6

2 tbsp olive oil

2 red onions, sliced

*1kg fresh tomatoes or 2 x
   400g tinned tomatoes*

*2 medium potatoes, peeled
   and chopped*

3 cloves garlic, crushed

2 tbsp tomato purée

1 tbsp brown sugar

1 litre Marigold bouillon

25g fresh basil

Salt and pepper

200g crème fraîche

Chives, chopped

WHEN TOMATOES ARE IN SEASON take advantage of them and use fresh; in the middle of winter, when they're not so good, a quality tinned tomato will suffice.

▬

If using fresh tomatoes - roast them in the oven for 20 minutes at 200°C/gas mark 6 with the red onions, garlic and a good glug of olive oil until soft and the skins fall away.

Transfer the tomatoes and onions to a large pot, add the potatoes, tomato purée and brown sugar. Stir well and pour over the stock. Bring to the boil and simmer, covered, for 20 minutes until the potatoes are soft.

Leave the soup to cool, add the fresh basil and blitz in a food processor until smooth. Return to the pan, season and serve hot with a spoonful of crème fraîche and fresh chives if you have them.

Or if using tinned tomatoes – heat the oil in a large pot over a low heat. Add the onions and potato and sprinkle in 1 teaspoon of salt. Cook very gently, stirring occasionally and then add the garlic. Add the tomatoes, purée and brown sugar. Stir well. Pour over the stock. Bring to the boil and simmer covered for 20 minutes until the potatoes are soft.

Leave the soup to cool, add the fresh basil and blitz in a food processor (or liquidize with a hand blender) until smooth. Return to the pan, season and serve hot with a spoonful of crème fraîche and fresh chives if you have them.

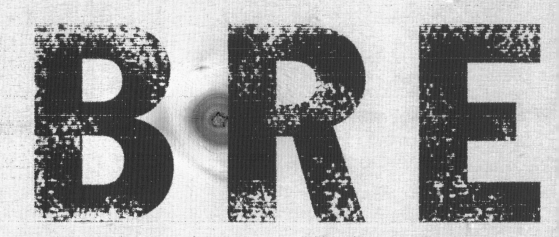

BRE

**OLIVE AND SUNBLUSHED TOMATO FOCACCIA
WITH CARAMELISED RED ONIONS**

HOMEMADE
BREAD

ADS

SEEDY CAFÉ BREAD   **WHITE BLOOMER**

WHAT COULD BE BETTER THAN
THE SMELL OF FRESH BAKED BREAD?

OLIVE AND SUNBLUSHED TOMATO FOCACCIA
WITH CARAMELISED RED ONIONS

Makes one large focaccia

850g strong white flour

130g mixed pitted olives,
  and sunblushed tomatoes,
  chopped

2 sachets of dried yeast (15g)
  or fresh if available

1 tsp salt

2 tbsp olive oil

2 red onions, sliced

600ml lukewarm water

THIS BREAD IS PERFECT for when you are having friends over and want to make something special.

—

Measure the flour in a large bowl. Make a well in the centre and add the yeast, salt, olive oil and water. Mix to form a sticky dough. If the dough is too dry add a little extra water.

Turn out onto a lightly floured surface and knead the dough for about 10 minutes, or until elastic and smooth.

Place in a lightly oiled bowl, cover with a clean tea towel or cling film and leave in a warm place for 1-1¼ hours until it has doubled in size.

Whilst bread is rising, caramelise red onions in a saucepan with a little olive oil, over a gentle heat, until soft with a slight crunch around the edges.

Lightly grease a baking sheet. Preheat oven to 200°C/gas mark 6. When the dough has risen, turn it out and knead for a further 2-3 minutes on a lightly floured surface and place on a baking sheet. With the tips of your fingers, poke holes in the dough. Sprinkle on red onions into the holes and push down. Zig zag with olive oil and scatter coarse salt on top.

Place on the middle shelf of the oven and bake for about 40-45 minutes until the bread has risen. It should sound hollow when tapped on the underside. If not, put it back in the oven for a further 5 minutes. Turn out onto a wire rack to cool.

SEEDY CAFÉ BREAD

Makes two 500g loaves

750g strong white flour
250g wholemeal flour
75g mix of sunflower,
* pumpkin seeds and pine*
* nuts (if feeling extravagant!)*
2 sachets of dried yeast (15g)
* or fresh if available*
1 tsp salt
2 tbsp olive oil
700ml lukewarm water

NOTHING BEATS HOMEMADE BREAD, and the joy of making it is great too! It is satisfying and incomparable to shop-bought bread. We always say that if we could make 20 loaves a day it would sell but the day would have to start too early! It can be tin-baked to give a traditional English shape or shaped as a free form oval.

—

Measure the flour and seeds into a large bowl. Make a well in the centre and add the yeast, salt and water. Mix to form a sticky dough. If the dough is too dry add a little extra water.

Turn out onto a lightly floured surface and knead the dough for about 10 minutes, or until elastic and smooth.

Place in a lightly oiled bowl, cover with a clean tea towel or cling film and leave in a warm place for 1-1¼ hours until it has doubled in size.

Lightly grease two loaf tins. Preheat oven to 200°C/gas mark 6. When the dough has risen, turn it out and knead for a further 2-3 minutes on a lightly floured surface and place in a loaf tin or on a baking sheet. Score the top roughly.

Place on the middle shelf of the oven and bake for about 40-45 minutes until the bread has risen. It should sound hollow when tapped on the underside. If not, put it back in the oven for a further 5 minutes. Turn out onto a wire rack to cool.

WHITE BLOOMER

Makes one large loaf

750g strong white flour

1 sachet of dried yeast (7g)
  or fresh if available

1 tsp salt

2 tbsp olive oil

500ml lukewarm water

A STRAIGHT FORWARD delicious white loaf. Similar to the seeded loaf, it can be tin-baked to give a traditional English shape or shaped as a free form oval.

—

Measure the flour into a large bowl. Make a well in the centre and add the yeast, salt and water. Mix to form a sticky dough. If the dough is too dry add a little extra water.

Turn out onto a lightly floured surface and knead the dough for about 10 minutes, or until elastic and smooth.

Place in a lightly oiled bowl, cover with a clean tea towel or cling film and leave in a warm place for 1-1¼ hours until it has doubled in size.

Lightly grease a baking sheet. Preheat oven to 200°C/gas mark 6. When the dough has risen, turn it out and knead for a further 2-3 minutes on a lightly floured surface and place on a baking sheet. Score the top roughly.

Place on the middle shelf of the oven and bake for about 40-45 minutes until the bread has risen. It should sound hollow when tapped on the underside. If not, put it back in the oven for a further 5 minutes. Turn out onto a wire rack to cool.

SALADS
PÂTÉS
& DIPS

SALADS
Pâtés & Dips

MISTLEY QUAY DRESSING

BACON, AVOCADO AND PINE NUT SALAD
WITH YOGHURT AND GARLIC DRESSING

ESTHER'S CRUNCHY COLESLAW

HERBY COUSCOUS

PRAWN AND AVOCADO SALAD

ROASTED VEGETABLE AND FETA SALAD

WARM BEETROOT, GOAT'S CHEESE AND PUY LENTIL
SALAD WITH LEMON AND HONEY DRESSING

CHICKEN LIVER PÂTÉ · GUACAMOLE · HOUMOUS
MUSHROOM PÂTÉ · SMOKED MACKEREL PÂTÉ

MISTLEY QUAY DRESSING

Makes 500ml dressing
1 tbsp demerara sugar
1 tbsp wholegrain mustard
3 large cloves garlic, crushed
150ml balsamic vinegar
200ml good quality olive oil
150ml sunflower oil
Salt and pepper

Mix the sugar, wholegrain mustard and garlic together in a large measuring jug. Then add the liquids starting with the balsamic vinegar, then olive and sunflower oils. Season well. Pour generously over a green salad.

BACON, AVOCADO AND PINE NUT SALAD WITH YOGHURT AND GARLIC DRESSING (GF)

Serves 4-6

250g bacon lardons
2 ripe avocados
250g mixed salad leaves
2 little gem lettuce
1 red onion, sliced
50g pine nuts

Dressing:
200ml natural yoghurt
4 tbsp mayonnaise
2 garlic cloves, crushed
1 lemon, juice and zest

Fry bacon off in a frying pan until crisp (this will take 5-7 minutes). Drain on kitchen paper.

Wipe frying pan with paper and fry off pine nuts until brown. Add a little olive oil to the pan and caramelise the red onion until soft and translucent.

Halve avocados and cut into thick slices, cover with lemon juice if not using immediately.

Make dressing by combining the yoghurt, mayonnaise, garlic and lemon zest and juice in a bowl. Taste, and season with salt and pepper.

Separate the little gem and mix with the other leaves. Place leaves in a serving bowl, sprinkle on the avocado, bacon, pine nuts and red onion. Drizzle with the garlic yoghurt dressing.

ESTHER'S CRUNCHY COLESLAW (GF)

Serves 6

3 carrots, coarsely grated

¼ red cabbage, thinly sliced

¼ white cabbage, thinly sliced

Salt and pepper

Handful sultanas

Handful mixed seeds

4 tbsp mayonnaise

ESTHER'S BEST CRUNCHY COLESLAW is a great accompaniment to a fresh summer quiche or with a jacket potato in the winter.

—

In a large bowl, mix together the grated carrots, cabbage, sultanas and mixed seeds. Stir through the mayonnaise. Add a little extra mayonnaise if needed to coat the carrots and cabbage.

Season to taste with salt and pepper.

The coleslaw can be made 2-3 hours before needed. Simply cover and chill until required.

HERBY COUSCOUS

Serves 4-6

250g couscous

50g sultanas

3 tbsp olive oil

1 tbs Marigold bouillon

1 lemon, zest and juice

1 teaspoon cumin

75g pine nuts

2 red onions

2 cloves garlic

1 red chilli

2 tbsp flat leaf parsley

1 tbsp basil

1 tbsp mint

Extra virgin olive oil,
  for drizzling

Salt and pepper

COUSCOUS IS AN ACCOMPANIMENT to any of our Middle Eastern dishes or makes a great salad in its own right with some grilled chicken or fish. You can alter the herbs and spices that you flavour the couscous with.

Place the couscous, 1 tablespoon olive oil, bouillon, lemon zest and juice in a large heatproof bowl. Use a fork to turn the couscous. Pour on 450ml boiling water, cover with a tea towel and large plate and set aside for 10 minutes or so.

Brown off pine nuts in a frying pan.

Meanwhile, place onion, garlic, chilli and herbs in the food processor. Pulse well until mixed. Then add mixture, sultanas and pine nuts to couscous and mix well. Drizzle with olive oil.

PRAWN AND AVOCADO SALAD Ⓖ🇪

Serves 4

2 avocados, sliced

200g tiger prawns,
   defrosted if frozen

2 lemons

250g green leaves,
   watercress and
   spinach is good

For the dressing:

2 tbsp mayonnaise

200ml natural yoghurt

1 tbsp tomato ketchup

2 cloves garlic, crushed

1 lemon, zest and juice

Few drops Tabasco

Salt and pepper

A SIMPLE BUT MOUTH WATERING and fresh summer salad, great when you have some ripe avocados that need using up!

—

To make the dressing, place the mayonnaise, natural yoghurt, ketchup, garlic, tabasco, lemon zest and juice in a large bowl and mix until well combined. Season to taste with salt and pepper.

Mix defrosted prawns well through sauce.

On a big white plate layer leaves followed by prawns and slices of avocado.

ROASTED VEGETABLE AND FETA SALAD ⓖⒻ

Serves 4

2 tbsp olive oil

1 aubergine, cubed

1 red pepper, sliced

1 yellow pepper, sliced

2 courgettes, sliced

2 carrots, cut into batons

1 red onion, sliced

1 tsp chopped thyme

250g feta cheese, cubed

100g mixed seeds toasted

250g of mixed salad

Salt and pepper

Preheat the oven to 200°C/gas mark 6.

Place the prepared vegetables in a large roasting tin, drizzle over the oil and sprinkle over the thyme. Season well.

Cook in the oven for 45 minutes until tender and beginning to brown.

Serve on a pile of fresh green leaves with feta cheese and toasted seeds and our Mistley Quay dressing.

Tip: Halloumi would make a good alternative to feta. It is a mild, salty Greek-style cheese that fries and grills well and keeps its shape while cooking.

WARM BEETROOT, GOAT'S CHEESE AND PUY LENTIL
SALAD WITH LEMON AND HONEY DRESSING ⓖⒻ

Serves 4

For the salad:

250g salad leaves

400g raw beetroot,
   peeled and cut into chunks

2 tbsp runny honey

2 tbsp balsamic vinegar

2 tbsp olive oil

200g puy lentils

2 tbsp Marigold bouillon

1 red onion, chopped finely

Handful flat leaf parsley,
   chopped finely

200g goat's cheese, cut into
   thick slices

Salt and pepper

For the dressing:

150ml olive oil

70ml white wine vinegar

1 tbsp runny honey

1 lemon, zest and juice

2 cloves garlic, crushed

A SIMPLE BUT IMPRESSIVE SALAD, perfect for a summer's lunch or supper.

———

Preheat the oven to 200°C/gas mark 6. Toss beetroot chunks in honey, olive oil, balsamic vinegar and seasoning. Place on a baking tray and roast in oven for about an hour until translucent and soft. Test by placing a fork into it.

In a small jug, assemble the ingredients for the dressing and mix well.

Cover puy lentils with water in a medium saucepan. Add 2 tbs bouillon to the water. Bring to the boil and then simmer for about 40 minutes until soft to touch but with an *al dente* crunch. Strain and place in a bowl. Whilst still warm, add enough dressing to coat them, then add red onion, and chopped parsley.

Take a frying pan and sprinkle a few drops of olive oil. Place goat's cheese in pan and cook until browned and soft. Place salad leaves on plate then arrange beetroot, puy lentils and warm goat's cheese on top. Spoon over remaining honey dressing.

Delicious!

CHICKEN LIVER PÂTÉ ⓖⒻ

Makes approximately
6 ramekins

*400g chicken livers,
trimmed and rinsed*

*125g butter, plus 50g for
top of pâté*

2 cloves garlic, crushed

1 tsp fresh thyme leaves

pinch of grated nutmeg

2 tbsp brandy

1½ tbsp redcurrant jelly

Salt and pepper

Few sprigs fresh thyme

RICHARD MAKES THIS VERY TASTY PÂTÉ and it is always enjoyed, simply serve it with some home-made brown toast.

—

Melt the butter in a large frying pan over a medium heat. Add the garlic and stir until softened. Add the chicken livers and the fresh thyme leaves. Stir frequently, for about 3 minutes, or until the livers are coloured on the outside but pink in the centre. Pour in the brandy, cook for a further 10 minutes before transferring the mixture to a food processor.

Add the redcurrant jelly to the livers and blend in a food processor until really smooth. Add the nutmeg and season well to taste. Spoon the pâté into 4-6 ramekins or one large terrine dish and cool in the fridge until completely cold.

Pour the melted butter over the pâté. Cover and refrigerate for at least 2-3 hours before eating. Garnish with a small spoonful of redcurrant jelly and sprig of thyme.

GUACAMOLE Ⓖ🇫

Makes one large bowl

2 large ripe avocados
2 cloves garlic, peeled
1 tomato
2 tbsp natural yoghurt
½ tsp dried chilli or small piece of fresh chilli
1 lemon, juice
Salt and pepper

Place all the ingredients in a food processor and, using the pulse action, process the mixture in short bursts until just combined. Season with salt and pepper.

Serve with warmed pitta bread.

HOUMOUS ⒼⒻ

Serves 4-6

2 onions, finely chopped

4-6 tbsp olive oil

2 cloves garlic, crushed

½ tsp cumin

½ tsp turmeric

1 lemon, zest and juice

100g natural yoghurt

425g tinned chickpeas,
  drained and rinsed

Salt and pepper

THIS IS A TANGY HOUMOUS which would be perfect for a summer's picnic. To save time we always use tinned chickpeas rather than dried and the result is just as delicious.

———

Heat 2 tablespoons of the olive oil in a frying pan and gently fry the onions with the garlic, cumin and turmeric until the onion softens.

Place the chickpeas, onion mixture and lemon zest and juice in a food processor. Add 2 tablespoons of olive oil and blend until smooth. You may need to add more olive oil if the houmous is too thick. Season to taste.

Drizzle with olive oil. Serve with warm pitta bread.

It is also very tasty with sweet chilli sauce poured on top. Store for up to 1 week, covered in a fridge.

Tip: You can always add some good quality red peppers from a jar to make an alternative houmous or add fresh coriander and extra lemon.

MUSHROOM PÂTÉ (GF)

Serves 6

50g butter

400g chopped mushrooms
  (ideally a few types combined)

2 garlic cloves, crushed

1 tbsp lemon juice

150g soft cream cheese

Handful flat leaf parsley

Salt and pepper

THIS IS SUCH A STRAIGHTFORWARD yet delicious pâté for a starter or lunch with some fresh bread and salad. It came from a wonderful lady who taught me so much called Julia Harvey. I can't thank her enough for all her inspiration and ideas.

Melt 50g butter in a large frying pan. Add the chopped mushrooms and garlic. Cook until mushrooms have softened and the liquid has evaporated.

Allow to cool, then process with the lemon juice, cream cheese and parsley. Process until smooth. Season to taste then spoon into ramekins or serving bowl.

Cover and chill for 2 hours. DELICIOUS and obviously incredibly simple!

SMOKED MACKEREL PÂTÉ ⒢

Serves 6

4 smoked mackerel fillets,
  skinned
200g cream cheese
3 tsp horseradish sauce
1 lemon, zest and juice
Small handful flat leaf
  parsley, chopped
Salt and pepper

A DELICIOUS and very straightforward pâté that makes a good starter or summer lunch served with brown toast and wedges of lemon.

———

Place all the ingredients, except the salt and pepper, in a food processor and using the pulse action process the mixture in short bursts until just combined.

Season well with salt and pepper. Taste and add more lemon juice if required.

Serve with toast or crackers.

FISH

FISH CAKES

MISTLEY QUAY FISH PIE

SMOKED HADDOCK, CHORIZO AND CANNELLINI BEAN HOTPOT

SMOKED HADDOCK CHOWDER

SMOKED SALMON & HORSERADISH WRAP

SPICED VEGETABLE AND PRAWN PILAU

MEAT

BACON & LEEK RISOTTO

CHICKEN, LEEK AND PARSLEY PIE

HEARTY BEEF STEW

PORK, APPLE AND CIDER MEATBALLS

SPICY LAMB TAGINE

SPICY MOROCCAN LAMB MEATBALLS IN TOMATO SAUCE

MAIN C

TARTS

ASPARAGUS TART

BACON, RED ONION AND TOMATO
OPEN TART

LEEK AND GOAT'S CHEESE TARTS

ROASTED BUTTERNUT SQUASH,
THYME AND PARMESAN TART

SMOKED SALMON AND
SPINACH TART

VEGETARIAN

AUBERGINE MOUSSAKA

CURRIED PARSNIP BAKE

MOROCCAN SPICED PIE

MOROCCAN VEGETABLE STEW

ROASTED VEGETABLE LASAGNE

VEGGIE SHEPHERD'S PIE

OURSES

FISH CAKES

Serves 4

350g potatoes, peeled and
  cut into chunks
30g butter
650g any cooked white fish,
  flaked
6 spring onions, finely chopped
2 tbsp fresh herbs, chives,
  parsley or basil
1 tbsp lemon juice
1 egg yolk
Salt and pepper
150g plain flour
1 egg, beaten
125ml milk
80g dry breadcrumbs
Olive oil to fry

THESE FISH CAKES come from our favourite little book by David Herbert called 'Complete Perfect Recipes'.

—

Place the potatoes in a large saucepan of salted water. Bring to the boil and cook for 20-25 minutes, or until tender. Drain and return to the saucepan. Cook over a low heat for 1-2 minutes to remove any remaining moisture. Mash well with the butter and leave to cool for 5 minutes.

In a mixing bowl, combine the mashed potato, fish, spring onions, herbs, egg yolk, lemon juice and season well.

Press the mixture into eight patties. Lightly coat each fishcake in the flour and shake off any excess.

Whisk together the beaten egg and milk in a shallow bowl. Place the breadcrumbs in a second shallow bowl.

Dip each fishcake into the egg mixture and then into the breadcrumbs, making sure each is well coated. Refrigerate for 20 minutes, or until ready to cook.

Heat the oil in a frying pan over a medium heat. Cook the fish cakes in batches if necessary, for 3-4 minutes on each side, or until golden.

Serve with lemon wedges, mayonnaise and a fresh green salad.

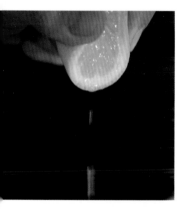

MISTLEY QUAY
CAFÉ

01206 393 884

DiCarlo
OLIO
EXTRAVERGINE
di OLIVA

MISTLEY QUAY FISH PIE

Serves 6

1.2kg potatoes, peeled and
  cut into medium chunks
75g butter
150ml milk
750g fish pie mix (cod, salmon,
  hake etc.)
250g undyed smoked haddock,
  skinned
150g peeled prawns
3 eggs, boiled and quartered
3 tbsp flat leaf parsley, chopped
Salt and pepper

White Sauce:
125g butter, melted
125g plain flour
750ml milk
150g grated cheese
Bay leaf
Salt and pepper

THIS IS ALWAYS A FRIDAY LUNCH SPECIAL and weekend winner, good accompanied by a glass of chilled white wine. Buy the best prawns you can afford - finding big juicy ones in your pie is such a treat!

———

Preheat oven to 180°C/gas mark 4.

Place the potatoes in a large pan of salted water. Bring to the boil and cook for 20-25 minutes until tender. Drain. Heat milk over medium heat and then mash potatoes with the butter and milk. Season with salt and pepper and leave in pan until needed.

Place the butter in a medium-sized saucepan and melt on a gentle heat. Mix in the flour, cook for 1 minute and then slowly pour in the milk, stirring constantly and adding more if needed. Stir until thickened and season with salt and pepper. Remove from the heat and set aside.

Place fish pie mix, prawns and haddock, into a large bowl. Add eggs, parsley and prawns to the fish. Combine white sauce with mixture and season well. Spoon mixture into a large ovenproof dish. Top with the mashed potato, fluff up with a fork, and dot with knobs of butter and sprinkle grated cheese on top.

Bake for 50-60 minutes until golden and bubbling.

SMOKED HADDOCK, CHORIZO AND CANNELLINI BEAN HOTPOT ⓖⒻ

Serves 4-6

2 tbsp olive oil

2 onions, sliced

2 cloves garlic, crushed

2 sticks celery, thinly sliced

Sprigs of rosemary

2 x 400g tin tomatoes

2 tbsp tomato purée

1 x 400g tin cannellini beans

300g chorizo, diced

2 tbsp fish stock

1 bay leaf

400g smoked haddock,
  skinned and cut into chunks

Salt and pepper

2 tbsp chopped
  flat-leaf parsley

100ml natural yoghurt, for
  topping

THIS IS SUCH A GOOD SUPPER, created by my wonderful sister Iona, who has it ready in about 15 minutes. Simple, tasty, and will impress friends!

—

Heat the oil in a large pot over a low heat. Add the onion, bay leaf, celery, rosemary and garlic. Cook gently over medium heat for about 10 minutes. Add the tinned tomatoes, tomato purée and bouillon. Add chorizo then cannellini beans. You are looking for a thick and rich sauce. Simmer for 5 minutes before placing haddock on top and gently poaching. Remove bay leaf and rosemary.

Serve in individual bowls with a dollop of yoghurt and a generous handful of flat-leaf parsley on top.

Delicious with fresh crusty loaf and green salad.

SMOKED HADDOCK CHOWDER (GF)

Serves 6

2 tbsp olive oil

1 onion, sliced

2 leeks, washed & sliced

2 sticks celery, thinly sliced

2 cloves garlic, crushed

3 medium-sized potatoes,
  peeled & diced into small
  cubes

1 litre fish stock

125ml white wine

1 bay leaf

Sprig of thyme

750g smoked haddock,
  skinned and cut into chunks

142ml carton single cream

Salt and pepper

2 tbsp chopped flat-leaf
  parsley

DELICIOUS ON A WINTER'S DAY!

—

Heat the oil in a large pot over a low heat. Add the onion, leeks, celery, potato and garlic. Cook gently over a medium heat for about 5 minutes. Add the hot stock, white wine, bay leaf and thyme. Bring to the boil and simmer for 10-15 minutes until the potatoes are soft. Remove bay leaf and thyme.

Add the fish to the saucepan and simmer for about 5 minutes until the fish is opaque. You can add some prawns too if you fancy being extravagant!

Stir in the cream and heat slowly without bringing to the boil. Sprinkle over the parsley and serve with a hunk of fresh crusty bread.

SMOKED SALMON AND HORSERADISH WRAP

Serves 4

4 tortilla wraps

200g rocket

1 tbsp horseradish

2 tbsp créme fraîche

1 lemon, zest and juice

200g best quality smoked
  salmon

Salt and pepper

EVER SINCE we started using Sladbury's smoked salmon from a local smokery in Walton-on-Naze we have had endless comments about our smoked salmon.

—

Make the mix; in a small bowl mix the horseradish, créme fraîche and lemon zest.

Lay a tortilla flat down, spread the horseradish mixture followed by a generous handful of rocket. Finish by placing slices of smoked salmon on the salad, a good squeeze of lemon and coarse ground black pepper.

Roll up and cut into 3 on the diagonal for a healthy and delicious lunch!

SPICED VEGETABLE AND PRAWN PILAU ⓖⓕ

Serves 4-6

2 leeks, washed trimmed and
   chopped
2 carrots, finely chopped
150g fresh or frozen peas
2 cloves garlic, crushed
4 tbsp vegetable oil
1 tsp garam masala
   (or ½ tsp cumin and ½ tsp
   ground coriander)
1 tsp turmeric
½ tsp cayenne pepper
Pinch chilli powder
350g basmati rice
400ml Marigold bouillon
100g raisins
50g desiccated coconut
400g fresh or frozen prawns

Dip:

125g tub natural yoghurt
¼ cucumber, grated
2 cloves garlic, crushed

AN EASY RECIPE which makes a good family dish. It only needs a few vegetables and spices, great if you have some prawns to use up, as it only needs store cupboard ingredients. If cooking this for children perhaps leave out the cayenne pepper and if you like it quite hot then add another teaspoon for that extra kick!

——

First prepare all the vegetables and garlic. Chop as finely as possible. If I am doing this for a large number of people I whizz them up in the food processor.

In a large heavy saucepan, heat the oil. Add the spices and fry for a couple of minutes. Add the vegetables and rice and fry the mixture for a further 5 minutes.

Add half the stock, bring to the boil and then cook over a gentle heat for 25-30 minutes until the rice is tender. Stir occasionally to avoid the rice from sticking and add a little stock if you think it needs some more liquid during the cooking time. Meanwhile mix the ingredients for the dip in a small bowl and set aside.

During the last 5 minutes of cooking stir in the raisins and prawns and season to taste. Stir in the coconut, or if you prefer, sprinkle over the top.

Transfer to a warm serving dish and serve straight away with the yoghurt dip.

BACON AND LEEK RISOTTO ⓖⒻ

Serves 4-6

50g butter

8 smoked streaky bacon
  rashers, chopped

3 large leeks, chopped

1 onion, finely chopped

2 garlic cloves, crushed

300g Arborio rice

125ml dry white wine

1.5 litres chicken stock

50g parmesan, grated

1 bunch chives, chopped

100ml single cream

Salt and pepper

RISOTTOS ARE EASY to prepare and make a lovely dish for friends round a table. I do par cook them and then finish it off at the last minute and don't think it affects the taste or texture. Simply take the risotto to half way through, cover with foil and finish cooking when you are ready to eat.

—

Bring the stock to a gentle simmer in a large saucepan.

Heat the butter in a large heavy-based saucepan and fry the bacon until crisp, remove from the pan and place on a plate with kitchen roll to drain off any excess fat.

Stir in the onion, leeks and garlic and soften for about 5 minutes. Add the rice and cook for 1 minute. Pour in the wine and keep stirring until it is absorbed.

Add the stock, one ladle at a time, stirring and waiting for the rice to absorb the liquid before you add more. Continue for about 20 minutes until the rice is just cooked and the risotto has a creamy consistency.

Season, then stir through the bacon and cream along with most of the Parmesan and chives, saving a little of each to scatter before serving.

CHICKEN, LEEK AND PARSLEY PIE

Serves 6

1kg chicken pieces

3 cloves garlic, peeled

3 good-sized leeks, washed,
   trimmed into 1cm pieces

1 onion, chopped

3 tsp plain flour

1 tsp curry powder

450ml milk

250ml chicken stock

Freshly ground pepper

2 tbsp parsley, finely chopped

500g ready-made puff pastry

Milk for glazing

S O TASTY, and a real family dish that everyone will like. Thanks Polly, for this recipe.

—

Preheat oven to 200°C/gas mark 6. Heat the oil in a large saucepan. Add the sliced leeks, chopped onion and garlic and cook gently for about 10 minutes, when the onions should be soft and transparent. Add the chicken pieces and stir well. Cook for about 15 minutes until chicken is tender. Stir in the curry powder and the flour. Cook for 1-2 minutes longer, then gradually stir in the milk and the chicken stock, stirring until the sauce boils. Season with salt and pepper. Stir in the finely chopped parsley. Place the chicken and leek mixture in the pie dish and make sure the sauce is spread evenly.

Roll out the puff pastry and use it to cover the pie. Decorate the pie with pastry leaves and brush the surface all over with milk. Bake in a hot oven for 20 minutes at 220°C/gas mark 7, then lower the heat to 180°C/gas mark 4, and cook for a further 20 minutes, or until the pie is golden brown.

HEARTY BEEF STEW Ⓖⓕ

Serves 4-6

1.2kg stewing steak, cut into
  2cm cubes

2 tbsp olive oil

2 large onions, chopped

2 cloves garlic, crushed

3 carrots, chopped

2 sticks celery, chopped

150g button mushrooms

1 litre beef stock

250ml red wine

1 x 400g can chopped
  tomatoes

4 sprigs thyme

1 bay leaf

2 tbsp flat leaf parsley, chopped

Salt and pepper

A GREAT RECIPE FOR ALL THE FAMILY and a good way of getting the children to eat their veg.

—

Heat the olive oil in a large casserole over a medium heat. Fry off the onions and garlic for 2 minutes. Then add the carrot and celery and cook, stirring occasionally for 5 minutes, or until the onion is tender.

Add the beef to the casserole dish, lightly brown for about 5 minutes, and then add the beef stock, red wine, tomatoes, button mushrooms, thyme, bay leaf and parsley. Bring to the boil. Cover and leave for at least 2 hours on a gentle heat, alternatively the dish can be placed in the oven at 150°C/gas mark 2, to cook. Stir the meat occasionally as it cooks.

Remove from the hob or oven and check the sauce. Add a little water if it appears too dry, or if watery, uncover and return to the oven to allow the sauce to reduce. Season well and serve with mash or a jacket potato.

Tip: If serving with mash try adding two tablespoons of wholegrain mustard and some cream.

PORK, APPLE AND CIDER MEATBALLS

Serves 4-6

700g pork mince

1 large apple, grated

2 leeks, chopped

3 cloves garlic

Good handful flat leaf parsley

Cider sauce:

1 large onion, chopped

3 garlic cloves, chopped

Small bottle of cider

200ml créme fraîche

150ml double cream

WONDERFUL DEBBIE created this recipe very recently and I think they are to die for!

—

Preheat oven to 180°C/gas mark 4.

Place the leek, garlic and parsley into a food processor and pulse until smooth. Take out and place in a large bowl with the pork mince and grated apple. Mix well.

Roll the pork mince between your palms to make about 20 small meatballs, roughly 2.5cm wide is a good size. Place on a non stick baking sheet and cook for about 20 minutes until browned.

Place the onion and garlic in a heavy based saucepan. Cook until soft and then add the cider. Bring to the boil, then reduce the heat and simmer gently for about 15 minutes. Add créme fraîche and cream. Stir well and then add parsley.

Purée the mixture until smooth with a hand held mixer. Add pork meatballs and their juices to sauce. Stir well and serve hot with basmati rice.

SPICY LAMB TAGINE ⓖⒻ

Serves 6

1kg lamb, cut into 2.5cm cubes

2 tbsp olive oil

2 onions, finely chopped

2 cloves garlic, crushed

4 carrots, finely chopped

2 celery stalks, finely chopped

1 tsp ground ginger

1 tsp cinnamon

1 tsp ground coriander

1 tsp chilli powder

2 bay leaves

2 x 400g tins chopped
   tomatoes

2 tbsp tomato purée

500ml lamb or beef stock

200g dried apricots, chopped

Handful fresh coriander,
   chopped

100g flaked almonds, lightly
   toasted

L IKE ALL STEWS, this benefits from being prepared
a day or two in advance to let the flavours mellow
and mingle.

———

Preheat oven to 160°C/gas mark 3.

Heat the oil in a large casserole dish, sauté the onions
and garlic until soft and lightly coloured. Add the carrot and
celery and stir for a several minutes.

Stir in the spices and cook until they begin to release
their aromas for about 1-2 minutes. Add the lamb pieces,
tomatoes and tomato purée.

Stir well and then add the bay leaves and apricots. Add
just enough stock to cover and season with salt and pepper.
Bring to the boil, then reduce to a simmer and cook in the
oven for about 1½-2 hours either on the hob or in the oven at
150°C/gas mark 2. By the end of the cooking time the meat
should be coated in a thick and glossy sauce.

Sprinkle with plenty of chopped coriander and the toasted
almonds. Serve with herb couscous.

SPICY MOROCCAN LAMB MEATBALLS
IN TOMATO SAUCE ⓖⒻ

Serves 4-6

700g lamb mince

1 large or 2 small red onions

3 cloves garlic, peeled

Small bunch of fresh coriander

2 tbsp fresh mint

1 tsp paprika

1 tsp cumin

1 tsp coriander

Tomato Sauce:

2 tsp olive oil

2 garlic cloves, chopped

2 x 400g tinned tomatoes

1 tbsp tomato purée

1 tbsp Marigold bouillon

Salt and pepper

Preheat oven to 180°C/gas mark 4.

Place the onion, garlic, coriander, mint and spices into a food processor and pulse until smooth. Take out and place in a large bowl with the lamb mince. Mix well.

Roll the lamb mince between your palms to make about 20 small meatballs, roughly 2.5cm wide is a good size. Place on a non stick baking sheet and cook for about 20 minutes until browned.

To make the sauce heat 2 tbsp olive oil in a non-stick pan. Add the garlic and sizzle gently for a couple of minutes. Tip in the tomatoes, purée, and bouillon, then simmer for 15 minutes until the sauce has thickened a little, squashing down the tomatoes as you cook.

Puree the mixture until smooth with a hand held mixer. Add lamb meatballs and their juices (pouring off any excess fat) to sauce. Stir well and serve with cous cous.

ASPARAGUS TART

Serves 6

500g ready-made shortcrust pastry
1 good-sized bundle asparagus
2 eggs
2 egg yolks
300ml double cream
150ml milk
100g grated parmesan
Salt and pepper

W E HAVE AMAZING ASPARAGUS in East Anglia and as soon as the first signs come out on the roadside, I go and stock up on bunches or my Mum will arrive with a handful. It is such a short season that one has to make the most of it, or it is over before you know it!

———

Preheat oven to 200°C/gas mark 6.

Prepare your asparagus, chop the stem to where it starts to feel woody and chop the wands into 2-3cm lengths. Steam the chopped stems before you throw the tender buds in after them: this avoids the mushiness of cooking them in together. Drain and leave to cool.

Roll out the pastry and line a 22cm flan tin, there's no need to trim off the excess at this stage. Line the pastry with greaseproof paper and fill with baking beans. Bake for 15 minutes, then remove the paper and beans and continue cooking until crisp and light golden. using a small, sharp knife, carefully trim off any excess pastry.

Whisk together the eggs, cream and milk, add the grated parmesan and season. Spoon the cooled asparagus into the pastry case, then pour over the egg mixture. Cook for 25-30 minutes, until puffed up and just set.

Leave to cool for 10 minutes. Try serving this with a fennel, orange and watercress salad. It will taste amazing!

BACON, RED ONION AND TOMATO OPEN TART

Serves 4-6

500g ready-made puff pastry

50g butter

4 tbsp double cream or
  créme fraîche

2 eggs, lightly beaten

8 smoked streaky bacon
  rashers, chopped

3 red onions, sliced

2 garlic cloves, chopped

1 handful fresh thyme

100g parmesan or gruyere,
  grated

4 firm ripe tomatoes, sliced
  (a serrated knife is best for
  this - try the tomato knife by
  Victorinox)

1 egg yolk, to glaze

Salt and pepper

A TASTY AND EASY LUNCH DISH suitable for carrying out triumphantly to the table, to your friends or family. For a more formal dinner party try individual tartlets; they're easier to serve.

—

Preheat oven to 200°C/gas mark 6.

Roll out the pastry on a lightly floured work surface to a rectangle about 30 by 40cm and about ½ cm thick. Line a baking sheet with parchment, transfer pastry to it, brush with egg yolk. Bake for 10 minutes or until golden brown and risen.

In a large frying pan add butter, fry off red onions and garlic until lightly coloured, add bacon pieces and cook until crispy. Place this mixture in a bowl with the cream, eggs, thyme and parmesan and mix well. Add salt and pepper.

Spread the mixture over the pastry. Arrange the tomato slices in rows down the length of the tart. Sprinkle with salt and pepper. Brush the folded over pastry border with egg glaze, then bake until the filling is puffed up and set and the pastry crisp and golden, 20-25 minutes. Drizzle the tomato slices with olive oil.

If making tartlets, cut 6 squares from your rolled out pastry, follow as above but reduce cooking time to 15-20 minutes.

Think ahead....bake up to 4 hours in advance. Reheat for 3 minutes in a 180°C oven/gas mark 4.

LEEK AND GOAT'S CHEESE TARTS

Serves 4

*250g ready-made shortcrust
pastry*

1 tbsp olive oil

2 leeks, cut into 1cm pieces

2 egg yolks

50ml double cream

100g black olives

2 tbsp fresh thyme

*100g soft rindless goat's
cheese, cubed*

Salt and pepper

BUY A SOFT RINDLESS GOAT'S CHEESE for this recipe. You can make them with any variation of the mixture. Very straightforward and versatile.

—

Preheat oven to 180°C/gas mark 4.

Roll out the pastry on a lightly floured surface and use to line four 12cm loose bottomed, fluted tart tins. Prick the pastry bases, line with greaseproof paper and fill with baking beans. bake for 12 minutes.

Meanwhile, heat the oil in a frying pan and and fry the leek until softened. Whisk the egg yolks in a bowl, stir in the cream, and then add the leek mixture. Mix well and fill each tart with the mixture. Scatter over the olives, thyme and goat's cheese.

Cook for 10-12 minutes, until the pastry is golden and the cheese is slightly melted.

Serve with fresh green leaves and buttered mint potatoes.

ROASTED BUTTERNUT SQUASH, THYME AND PARMESAN TART

Serves 6

500g ready-made shortcrust
  pastry
½ butternut squash,
  cut into chunks
Handful fresh thyme
2 red onions, cut into chunks
50g sun blushed tomatoes
2 cloves garlic
1 tbsp olive oil
4 eggs
150ml cream
150ml milk
100g grated parmesan
Salt and pepper

Preheat oven to 200°C/gas mark 6.

Place the butternut squash, onion and garlic over a baking sheet. Sprinkle with olive oil. Bake for 30-40 minutes until tender.

Roll out the pastry and line a 22cm flan tin, there's no need to trim off the excess at this stage. Line the pastry with greaseproof paper and fill with baking beans. Bake for 15 minutes, then remove the paper and beans and continue cooking until crisp and light golden. Using a small, sharp knife, carefully trim off any excess pastry.

Whisk together the eggs, cream and milk, parmesan and seasoning: the amount of liquid will depend on your tart tin so begin with the smaller amount and add more if it doesn't look like the mixture will fill the pastry case. Then add the thyme and squash mixture, mix well and pour into prepared pastry dish. Arrange sun blushed tomatoes on top and push down into mixture.

Bake for 35-40 minutes until just set, puffed up and deliciously browned.

Serve with crisp green leaves.

SMOKED SALMON AND SPINACH TART

Serves 6

500g ready-made shortcrust
 pastry
500g fresh spinach or frozen,
 thawed
300g smoked salmon,
 chopped
30g butter
1 tbsp olive oil
4 eggs
150ml cream
150ml milk
Salt and pepper

I SAID TO DEBBIE RECENTLY that a bag of frozen spinach was an essential for the freezer, you can make a breakfast with it with some eggs, a quick soup or use to make a delicious tart like this one. We are supplied with smoked salmon by a fabulous smokery called Sladbury's in Walton-on-the-Naze.

—

Preheat oven to 200°C/gas mark 6.

Roll out the pastry and line a 22cm flan tin, there's no need to trim off the excess at this stage. Line the pastry with greaseproof paper and fill with baking beans. Bake for 15 minutes, then remove the paper and beans and continue cooking until crisp and light golden. using a small, sharp knife, carefully trim off any excess pastry.

Heat the butter and olive oil in a saucepan and add spinach. (This can also be done in the microwave for quickness). Whisk together the eggs, cream, milk, and seasoning. Add the spinach and salmon to mixture and stir well. Pour the whole lot into the pastry case. Bake for 35-40 minutes until just set, puffed up and deliciously browned.

Serve with a tomato salad and fresh hunk of bread and butter.

AUBERGINE MOUSSAKA

Serves 6

3 tbsp olive oil

2 large aubergines, sliced into
  1.5cm slices

2 onions, finely chopped

3 cloves garlic, crushed

300g red lentils, rinsed

2 x 400g tinned tomatoes

2 tbsp tomato purée

1 tbsp Marigold bouillon

Cheese Sauce:

125g plain flour

125g butter

570ml milk

200g cheddar cheese, grated

A VERY GOOD VEGETARIAN DISH that is loved by veggies and meat eaters alike. The combination of slow cooked tomato and lentil sauce, soft aubergines and cheese sauce make a very good dish suitable for a special occasion or party. It would come to no harm in the fridge if made a couple of days before your event. If you have a good non-stick pan use it, as otherwise I find lentils have a tendency to stick to the bottom.

—

Preheat oven to 200°C/gas mark 6.

Arrange the aubergine slices on a baking tray and drizzle with olive oil. Bake in the oven for 40-45 minutes. Turn them half way through the cooking time. They should be soft and brown when cooked.

Whilst the aubergines are cooking, heat the oil in a large saucepan and add the onions and garlic. Cook over a moderate heat until soft. Add the lentils, tinned tomatoes, tomato purée, bouillon and season with salt and pepper. Bring to the boil and then simmer for about 30 minutes making sure the mixture doesn't stick during the cooking time.

Whilst the sauce is simmering, place another medium size saucepan on a gentle heat. Melt the butter, stir in the flour, cook for 1 minute and then slowly pour in the milk, stirring constantly. Stir until thickened. Add the cheddar cheese, reserving 50g to sprinkle over the top. *(continued over)*

Let the cheese melt into the sauce, season with salt and pepper and then remove from the heat.

Take a 20cm x 20cm ovenproof dish. Place the lentil mixture over the bottom, then layer the aubergines on top of this. Finish with a thick layer of cheese sauce and sprinkle with the remaining 50g of cheddar.

Bake for 30 minutes or until the moussaka is cooked. Cover with foil if the top becomes too brown during cooking.

Serve with a lightly dressed crispy green salad.

CURRIED PARSNIP BAKE

Serves 6

2 tbsp olive oil

1kg parsnips, peeled and
  chopped into 2cm pieces

1 large/2 small leeks, washed
  and chopped into 2cm pieces

2 cloves garlic, crushed

250g fresh tomatoes,
  chopped or tinned chopped
  tomatoes

2 tbsp tomato purée

500ml Marigold bouillon

2 tsp curry powder

Pinch cumin

Pinch turmeric

Pinch pepper

250g breadcrumbs

50g mixed seeds

50g cheddar, grated

Preheat oven to 200°C/gas mark 6.

In a medium sized saucepan sauté the onions, garlic and leeks in the olive oil until soft and golden.

Add the spices to the onion mixture and stir thoroughly. Add the parsnips, tomatoes and tomato purée. Add enough bouillon to cover. Cook the vegetables until tender.

Spoon the curried vegetables into a large dish. Cover with the breadcrumbs, mixed seeds and grated cheese.

Bake in the oven for 30 minutes, until golden and bubbling.

MOROCCAN SPICED PIE

Serves 6

2 tsp each coriander and
  cumin seeds
1 tsp paprika, extra for
  dusting
½ tsp ground cinnamon
150ml olive oil
900g squash, peeled,
  deseeded and cut into small
  chunks (about 2cm)
12 shallots, quartered
4cm piece root ginger, finely
  chopped
140g whole blanched almonds
140g shelled pistachios
75g dried cranberries
6 tbsp clear honey
225g fresh spinach
400g tinned chickpeas
2 garlic cloves
1 tsp ground cumin
3 tbsp lemon juice
4 tbsp fresh coriander, chopped
100g butter
8 large sheets filo pastry
Lemon wedges to serve

This pie came from the Good Food Magazine and is one we have used for a long time, due to the reason that it is so good. There are layers of delicious ingredients which put together make such a good combination. It does take some time to assemble but I can assure you it is well worth the effort. Good for a celebration meal or vegetarian option for Easter or Christmas.

—

Preheat oven to 200°C/gas mark 6.

Dry fry the seeds briefly in a small pan until toasty; don't let them burn. Grind coarsely using a pestle and mortar (or a bowl and the end of a rolling pin), then mix in the paprika, cinnamon, ½ tsp salt and 4 tbsp oil. Tip the squash into a roasting tin, pour over the spiced oil and toss. Roast for 20 minutes until brown and soft.

Meanwhile, heat 2 tbsp of oil in a frying pan, add the shallots and cook, stirring, until they start to brown. Stir in the ginger and 100g each almonds and pistachios. When brown, toss in the cranberries, 2 tbsp honey, and the spinach so it wilts. Take off the heat and stir into the squash, when it comes out of the oven. Set aside.

In a food processor, whizz the chickpeas with the garlic, cumin, remaining oil, lemon juice, 2 tbsp water and salt and pepper to make houmous. Stir in the coriander.

Melt the butter in a small pan. Put a loose-bottomed 28cm

Harissa Yoghurt Sauce:
200g Greek yogurt
6 tbsp milk
3 large sprigs mint, chopped
2-3 tbsp harissa paste

quiche tin on a baking sheet and brush with some butter. Keeping the filo covered with a damp cloth so it doesn't dry out, lay one sheet over half of the tin so that it hangs over the edge by about 10cm. Lay another sheet on the other side, so it overlaps the first in the centre and hangs over the opposite edge. Brush with butter. Lay two more filo sheets in the opposite direction in the same way and brush with more butter.

Build up two more layers in this way, so you use a total of eight sheets of filo. Pile half the squash mixture in the centre of the pastry. Spread over the houmous and then the rest of the squash mixture. One at a time, bring the edge of each filo sheet up to the centre to cover the filling, creating voluptuous folds as you go. Brush carefully with more butter. (If making a day ahead, cover now with cling film and chill. To reheat, remove the pie from the fridge, heat the oven, then bake for 35-40 minutes.)

Bake for 30-35 minutes, until crisp and golden. Just before the pie is ready, reheat any remaining butter in the pan, tip in the rest of the nuts and fry until golden. Spoon in the 4 remaining tbsps of honey and, when it melts, take off the heat and pour over the pie.

Serve with harissa yoghurt sauce (mix the yoghurt and milk together to make a thin sauce, stir in the herbs and season. Swirl in harissa to taste) and lemon wedges.

MOROCCAN VEGETABLE STEW ⓖⓕ

Serves 6

2 tbsp olive oil

2 onions, sliced

2 garlic cloves, crushed

1 aubergine, chopped

2 sweet potatoes, chopped

2 peppers, chopped

2 carrots, chopped

1 tsp ground cumin

1 tsp ground coriander

½ tsp turmeric

600ml vegetable stock

400g can chickpeas, drained
  and rinsed

4 tomatoes, chopped

A DISH LIKE THIS IS SO SIMPLE TO MAKE, chop away and before you know it your supper is ready!

—

Heat the oil in a medium saucepan. Add the garlic and onions and fry for 2-3 minutes until beginning to soften. Then stir in the spices,

Add the vegetables and fry for 3-4 minutes, then add the spices and cook for a further minute.

Pour the stock into the pan and bring to the boil. Reduce the heat and simmer for 15 minutes. Add the chickpeas and tomatoes and simmer for a further 5 minutes.

Serve with couscous, natural yoghurt and green salad for a tasty and healthy meal.

ROASTED VEGETABLE LASAGNE

Serves 6

2 tbsp olive oil

2 large red onions, chopped

4 cloves garlic, crushed

½ red chilli, chopped

2 x 400g cans chopped
  tomatoes

1 tbsp sugar

1 tbsp tomato purée

2 tbsp basil, finely chopped

1 aubergine, cut into chunks

2 carrots, cut into chunks

1 courgette, cut into chunks

1 red pepper, cut into chunks

12 button mushrooms

Salt and pepper

12 sheets dried lasagne,
  approx 250g

White Sauce:

125g butter

125g plain flour

570ml milk

150g cheddar cheese, grated

50g parmesan, grated

Salt and pepper

THIS IS A REAL WINTER WARMER at the café and always popular. If you can be creative when cutting the vegetables they will look better, courgettes on the diagonal for example.

—

Preheat oven to 180°C/gas mark 4.

Heat the oil in a large saucepan over a medium heat and sauté the onions, 2 cloves of crushed garlic and chilli for 5 minutes. Add the tomatoes, tomato purée and sugar and bring to the boil. Reduce the heat and simmer gently, stirring occasionally for 20 minutes, or until soft.

Meanwhile, place chopped vegetables for roasting and add 2 cloves crushed garlic into a large roasting tin, drizzle with oil and season. Cook in the oven for about 40 minutes until soft.

Place a medium sized saucepan on a gentle heat. Melt the butter, stir in the flour, cook for 1 minute and then slowly pour in the milk, stirring constantly. Add more milk if needed and stir until thickened. Add 100g of the cheddar cheese. Stir until thickened. Remove from the heat and set aside.

Add the cooked vegetables to the tomato sauce and stir well.

Take a large ovenproof dish and start by lightly covering the bottom with a thin layer of the cheese sauce. Then layer with tomato and vegetable sauce followed by lasagne sheets and lastly white sauce. Repeat the process again and finish with a good layering of white sauce and grated parmesan and cheddar. Don't overfill the dish as it can spill over.

Place the dish onto a baking tray to avoid spillages and bake in the oven for 30 minutes or until bubbling and cooked. Cover with foil if the top becomes too brown during cooking.

Serve with a crunchy green salad.

VEGGIE SHEPHERD'S PIE ⓖⒻ

Serves 6

1 tbsp olive oil

200g red lentils

1 large onion

2 cloves garlic, crushed

50g carrots

50g swede

50g celeriac

2 sticks celery

1 green pepper, deseeded

1 x 400g can chopped
  tomatoes

1 tbsp tomato purée

1 tbsp mixed dried herbs

800ml-1 litre Marigold bouillon

Salt and pepper

For the topping:

1kg potatoes, peeled

150ml milk, warmed

50g butter

100g cheddar, grated

USE WHATEVER VEGETABLES take your fancy-parsnip, courgettes, leeks, sweetcorn! It's a great vegetarian dish and meat-eaters really like it too.

—

Place the potato pieces in a large saucepan of salted water. Bring to the boil and cook for 20-25 minutes until tender.

Roughly chop all the vegetables before piling into the food processor and process until chopped small.

Heat some olive oil in a large saucepan over a medium heat. Add chopped vegetables and cook gently over a medium heat for 10-15 minutes, stirring now and then until they are soft and golden on the edges. Then add the lentils, herbs, tomato purée and chopped tomato and bouillon. Cook gently for 20-25 minutes until soft.

Pre-heat oven to 180°C/Gas Mark 4.

Drain and return potatoes to the saucepan. Cook over low heat for 1-2 minutes to remove any remaining moisture. Mash well with the milk and butter and season well.

Spoon the vegetable mixture into a baking dish and place mashed potato on top. Sprinkle with grated cheese and bake pie on top shelf until the top is lightly browned. This should take about 40 minutes.

PUDDINGS®

BRITISH CLASSICS
ESTHER'S BEST PUD RECIPES

11 AMAZING PUDDINGS

PERFECT FOR ANY OCCASION

APPROX. 4-6 SERVINGS
PER RECIPE

2012

APPLE CRUMBLE

APRICOT AND VANILLA TART

BERRY TRIFLE

BREAD & BUTTER PUDDING

CHOCOLATE ROULADE

JULIA'S TIRAMISU

LEMON MERINGUE PIE

MERINGUES

MILE HIGH BERRY PIE

MUM'S DATE, WALNUT AND HONEY TART

STICKY TOFFEE PUDDING
WITH BUTTERSCOTCH SAUCE

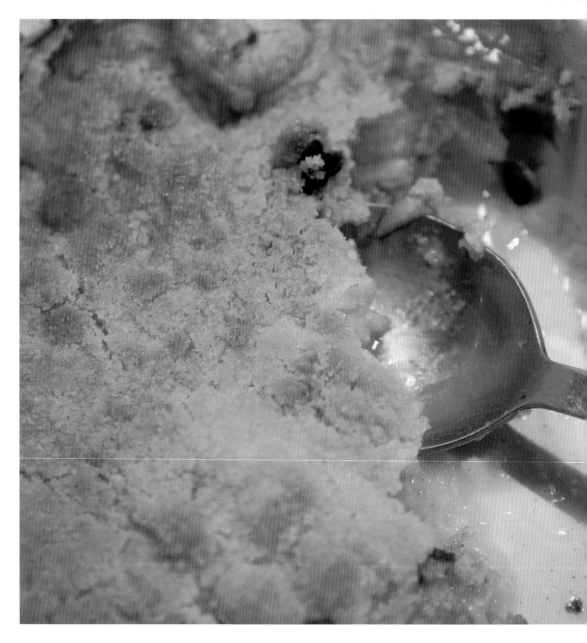

APPLE CRUMBLE

Serves 6

Fruit base:

1kg or 6 large cooking apples

1 lemon, zest and juice

100g sultanas

1 tsp cinnamon

175g caster sugar

Crumble topping:

200g plain flour

200g brown sugar + extra to
   sprinkle on top

150g chilled butter, diced

50g ground almonds

CRUMBLE IS ALWAYS POPULAR and just great when there is a glut of fruit and can be used to make a delicious pudding. Obviously this can be adapted to any seasonal fruit such as pear, plum or rhubarb.

I use the magimix to make the crumble. Once made and if you have time, put it in the freezer for a couple of hours. It makes the crumble crunchy and tasty once cooked!

—

Preheat the oven to 180°C/gas mark 4.

Peel core and chop the apples. Arrange evenly in a large baking dish. Mix in the lemon juice, rind, sultanas, cinnamon and sugar to the apples.

Either place your crumble ingredients into the food processor, or if doing by hand, use your fingertips to rub together the ingredients until the mixture resembles breadcrumbs and starts to clump together.

Sprinkle the crumble mixture evenly over the fruit and to finish sprinkle over extra brown sugar. Bake for 40 minutes, or until golden and bubbling.

Serve with custard, cream or ice cream.

APRICOT AND VANILLA TART

Serves 8

500g pack ready-made
  shortcrust pastry
400g apricots, fresh and pitted
  or tinned and drained
125g butter, softened
125g caster sugar
1 egg
1 egg yolk
Few drops of vanilla essence
30g plain flour
200g créme fraîche

A DELICIOUS SUMMER TART that also works well with tinned apricots. Thanks to Gaye Drummond.

—

Preheat the oven to 180°C/gas mark 4.

Roll out the pastry and line a 24cm flan tin, there's no need to trim off the excess at this stage. Line the pastry with greaseproof paper and fill with baking beans. Bake for 15 minutes, then remove the paper and beans and continue cooking until crisp and light golden. Using a small, sharp knife, carefully trim off any excess pastry.

Lay the apricots on top of the pastry.

Firstly mix the butter, sugar, egg, egg yolk and vanilla essence before adding the créme fraîche and flour. Beat both sets of ingredients together and then pour over the apricots.

Cook tart for 40-45 minutes until set but slightly wobbly.

Delicious with vanilla ice cream.

BERRY TRIFLE Ⓖ

Serves 6

300g berries, fresh or frozen and defrosted

150g sponge or Madeira cake cut into small pieces

150ml apple juice or something stronger if you prefer

500g carton custard

270ml double cream

Good quality chocolate shavings

E ITHER MAKE THIS IN A BOWL or if you have any Moroccan tea glasses these little puddings look very pretty in them. It is a very simple but effective pudding and any type of berry can be used.

This can be made in advance and kept chilled but add whipped cream just before serving.

—

Line your dish or individual glasses with pieces of the sponge. Pour over the liquid, either apple juice or your favourite liqueur or sherry!

Spoon the fruit over the sponge base, then follow with the custard.

Just before serving lightly whip the cream and then put on top of the trifle. Decorate with the chocolate shavings.

BREAD AND BUTTER PUDDING

Serves 6

8-10 slices white bread (either
 sliced or from an uncut loaf)
100g butter
2 tbsp good quality marmalade
50g caster sugar
1 tsp vanilla essence
4 eggs
Handful sultanas or raisins
400ml milk
200ml double cream
2 tbsp demerara sugar

THIS IS SUCH AN EASY winter recipe loved by most people. It is quite rich so if trying to watch your weight not a good one but that probably goes without saying! Great for a Sunday roast.

—

Butter the slices of bread. Brush with marmalade and cut diagonally into quarters. Arrange the bread in two layers in a deep ovenproof dish and sprinkle with the sultanas or raisins.

Whisk together the eggs, caster sugar, vanilla essence, milk and cream. Pour the mixture over the bread and sprinkle with the demerara sugar. Cover the bread, making sure it is well covered and add a little extra milk if necessary. Leave for 30 minutes to allow the bread to soak up the liquid and absorb the flavours.

Preheat the oven to 180°C. Place the dish in the hot oven and bake for 45-50 minutes until the custard is set and the bread is puffed and golden on top.

Tip: If you want to use any croissants that need eating up, or brioche, this recipe works very well for those too. Also hot cross buns around Easter time are a winner.

CHOCOLATE ROULADE Ⓖ🄵

Serves 6-8

6 eggs, separated

250g caster sugar

150g dark chocolate, broken
  into pieces

50g cocoa

¼ tsp vanilla essence

300ml double cream, whipped

Icing sugar or cocoa powder
  for dusting

THEY ARE LIGHT, KEEP WELL for a day or two and are gluten-free, which is helpful if you need a pudding that is without wheat but delicious at the same time!

———

Preheat the oven to 180°C/gas mark 4. Line a swiss roll tin with greaseproof paper and lightly oil.

Start by melting the chocolate over a pan of simmering water. Beat the egg whites first (saves you having to wash the whisks!) until stiff. In a separate bowl beat the sugar and eggs until thick and creamy. Mix in the vanilla essence. Add the cooled melted chocolate, sieve the cocoa in and fold in gently with a large metal spoon.

Pour the chocolate mixture into the prepared tin and cook for approximately 25 minutes. Cool in the tray for 5 minutes before peeling off the greaseproof paper.

Roll gently onto a fresh piece of greaseproof paper and then roll in a damp tea towel. Don't worry if it cracks, it is fairly versatile.

Roll out when cool and spread lashings of freshly whipped cream and fresh strawberries or raspberries.

Roll the roulade up and sprinkle with a dusting of either cocoa powder or icing sugar.

Serve with some raspberry or strawberry coulis.

JULIA'S TIRAMISU

Serves 6-8

3 eggs, separated

5 tbsp caster sugar

180ml double cream

250g mascarpone

250ml strong black coffee

125ml brandy, whisky or rum

175g sponge fingers or
  boudoir biscuits

75g dark chocolate, grated

Cocoa power, to dust

Large decorative bowl to serve

A SHOW-STOPPER OF A PUDDING, really decadent and gets better the longer it sits. Julia Harvey taught me the recipe, and also how to cook for big numbers on a small budget.

Take 4 bowls from your cupboard, 1 large and 3 small.

In your large bowl, beat the egg whites until still peaks form. In the next bowl beat the egg yolks and sugar until pale and thick. In the third bowl whisk the cream, and once whipped gradually fold in the mascarpone. Leave some lumps in it as it will give your pudding a more interesting texture. Combine the egg whites, egg yolks and cream in the large bowl.

Mix together the coffee and brandy in your fourth bowl and then pour into a flat bottomed dish. Dip half the biscuits into the coffee for a few seconds. Line the base of your dish. They will rapidly absorb the liquid, so only a very quick dip is needed. Do not let them go soggy.

Cover the biscuits with half the mascarpone mixture. Repeat with a layer of coffee-soaked biscuits and cover with the remaining mascarpone. Cover with cling film and refrigerate for at least 4 hours.

Just before serving, sprinkle with grated chocolate and dust with cocoa.

LEMON MERINGUE PIE

Serves 8

500g ready-made shortcrust
  pastry
2 tins condensed milk
3 eggs, separated
5 lemons, zest and juice
6 tbsp sugar

RICHARD IS A MASTER AT THIS PUDDING and it is truly sweet and delicious. Many ask what the secret ingredient is and I think that would have to be the condensed milk!

You will need a 24cm flan dish or small pastry tin.

—

Preheat oven to 190°C/gas mark 5.

Roll out the pastry and line a 24cm flan tin, there's no need to trim off the excess at this stage. Line the pastry with greaseproof paper and fill with baking beans. Bake for 15 minutes, then remove the paper and beans and continue cooking until crisp and light golden. Using a small, sharp knife, carefully trim off any excess pastry.

Combine the tins of condensed milk with the 3 egg yolks, grated zest and juice of the lemons. Pour into the baked pastry case. Bake for 10-15 minutes until lemon mixture is set.

Whisk the 3 egg whites until soft peaks form, gradually add the sugar. Place on top of the lemon mix and spoon neatly around, leaving 1cm of lemon showing.

Using a palette knife, comb the egg white mixture so you have peaks forming on top.

Bake in the oven for 15 minutes or until golden brown.

MERINGUES Ⓖ🅕

5 egg whites, room temperature
300g caster sugar

THIS RECIPE will make 8-10 large meringues, but would also make a good-sized pavlova, enough to feed 10 people.

—

Preheat the oven to 150°C/gas mark 2. Line two large oven trays with baking paper.

Place the egg whites in a large, clean, dry bowl. Whisk with an electric mixer or hand-held electric whisk for about 5 minutes until stiff peaks form. The mixture should cling to the beaters.

Continue to whisk the mixture, gradually adding the sugar 1 tablespoon at a time, beating well after each addition. Continue this process until the sugar has been added and your mixture is stiff and glossy – about 5 to 10 minutes.

Using two tablespoons, spoon the mixture onto the baking tray/s.

Bake the meringues for 1½ hours, or until pale and dry. Turn off the heat and allow to cool whilst still inside the oven.

Serve with freshly whipped cream and strawberries in the summer.

A good winter alternative is a coffee and nut cream. Melt 50g butter, add 2 tablespoons coffee extract, 75g toasted nuts and 125ml whipped double cream.

MILE HIGH BERRY PIE

Serves 6-8

300g ginger biscuits, crushed in a bag

100g butter, melted

120g caster sugar

2 large egg whites

Raspberries (about 350g)

285ml double cream

RICHARD MAKES THIS SPECIAL PUDDING in the summer and it is truly divine. It is worth waiting for raspberries to come into season as they are so much better than ones from afar or frozen!

Freeze a 22cm cake tin, preferably a spring-form if you have one and line the bottom and sides with baking paper.

Mix the crushed ginger biscuits with the melted butter and press into base of cake tin.

Combine the caster sugar, egg whites and raspberries into a large bowl and beat with an electric mixer until pale and slightly stiff.

Whip the cream lightly in a separate bowl, and then stir into the egg mixture. Spoon onto biscuit base and freeze overnight. Remove from tin and allow to defrost for about 1 hour, but don't leave out for too long as it will melt, especially on a warm day!

Decorate with raspberries and fresh mint.

MUM'S DATE, WALNUT AND HONEY TART

500g ready-made shortcrust
  pastry
100g unsalted butter
140g honey
100ml double cream
280g walnuts/chopped dates
140g caster sugar
5 egg yolks

A TRULY SCRUMPTIOUS and spoiling tart, which is perfect for a special lunch or dinner. Thanks Mum for this one!

—

Preheat the oven to 200°C/gas mark 6.

Roll out the pastry and line a 24cm flan tin, there's no need to trim off the excess at this stage. Line the pastry with greaseproof paper and fill with baking beans. Bake for 15 minutes, then remove the paper and beans and continue cooking until crisp and light golden. Using a small, sharp knife, carefully trim off any excess pastry.

Melt butter, honey and cream; be careful not to let this mixture get too hot. Add walnuts, chopped dates and sugar to butter mixture. When this has cooled add egg yolks.

Bake for 40-50 minutes until just set, puffed up and deliciously browned. Check the oven after 20 minutes and if necessary turn the temperature down. The tart will firm up as it cools. Allow cooling for at least 45 minutes before serving.

Serve with clotted cream or vanilla ice cream

STICKY TOFFEE PUDDING WITH BUTTERSCOTCH SAUCE

Serves 6

170g dates, pitted and
  chopped
1 tsp bicarbonate of soda
60g butter
170g caster sugar
2 medium eggs
170g self-raising flour
½ tsp vanilla essence

Butterscotch sauce:
200g brown sugar
125ml double cream
130g butter
½ tsp vanilla essence

THE BEST WINTER PUDDING, again from my friend and teacher Julia. It is fail proof and just so delicious that you have to try it!

—

Preheat oven to 200°C/gas mark 6, and grease an 18 x 28cm baking tin.

Pour 300ml boiling water over the dates, add the bicarbonate of soda and leave to sit for at least an hour.

Cream the butter and sugar together and then add the eggs one at a time and beat well.

Fold the flour into the butter mixture, and stir in the dates. Add vanilla essence and then pour into the tin.

Bake in the centre of the oven for 30-40 minutes. For the sauce combine the sugar, butter, cream and vanilla essence in a saucepan. Try not to stir. Bring to the boil, then reduce the heat and simmer gently.

Pour the sauce over the pudding or serve separately in a small jug.

CA

ESTHER'S BEST
CAKES

CARROT CAKE
CHEESE SCONES
CHOCOLATE & BEETROOT BROWNIES
CHOCOLATE CAKE
CLAUDIA RODEN'S ORANGE AND ALMOND CAKE
CRUNCHIE CHOCOLATE PEANUT BARS
CUPCAKES
FLAPJACKS
FRUIT SCONES
GINGER CAKE
LEMON DRIZZLE CAKE
MOIST FRUIT CAKE
SUGARLESS FRUIT CAKE

KES

CARROT CAKE

Makes 1 x 900g loaf
4 eggs, lightly beaten
375g demerara sugar
100ml vegetable oil
2 tbsp golden syrup
150g plain flour
150g self raising flour
1 tsp bicarbonate of soda
½ tsp ground cinnamon
2½ carrots, grated
60g pineapple, drained and
  crushed
60g walnuts or pecans
  chopped

Topping:
175g cream cheese
60g softened unsalted butter
375g icing sugar sifted
1 lemon, zest and juice

This is a winner of a cake and comes from David Herbert's 'Complete Perfect Recipes'. It is delicious, especially once you have made the very straight-forward cream cheese topping to go on top.

—

Preheat oven to 160°C/gas mark 2-3. Lightly grease and line a large 1kg loaf tin or use a liner.

In a large mixing bowl, lightly whisk together the eggs and sugar until the sugar has dissolved and the mixture is frothy. Stir in the oil and golden syrup and mix with a wooden spoon until smooth.

Sift the flours, bicarbonate of soda and the cinnamon into the egg mixture and mix until smooth. Stir in the carrot, pineapple and walnuts/pecans.

Spoon the mixture into the prepared tin and bake for 1-1¼ hours, or until a skewer placed into the cake comes out clean. Allow cake to cool down before turning out onto a wire rack.

To make the cream cheese topping, beat the cream cheese with the butter until combined. Continue to beat, gradually added the icing sugar, then mix in the lemon juice and zest. Carefully spread the topping over the cake and leave to set.

CHEESE SCONES

Makes 6-8

500g self raising flour

120g Stork margarine

1 tsp mustard powder

*Handful mature cheddar
  cheese, grated*

1 egg beaten with 125ml milk

Salt and pepper

Preheat oven to 200°C/gas mark 6 and lightly grease a baking sheet or line with baking parchment.

Place flour into a mixing bowl. Add the margarine and mix to a fine crumb mixture, with light fingers.

Add the mustard powder, grated cheese and seasoning, then carefully add the beaten egg and milk. Mix well with a large spoon or spatula. (Add liquid slowly as too much liquid tends to make the scones wet). You want to have a firm but light mixture.

Turn dough out onto a floured surface and pat the mixture down to the height of the cutter. Using a 6cm cutter cut out scones and put onto baking tray.

Brush with a little beaten egg. Top scones with some grated cheese and bake for 15-20 minutes until bubbling and golden.

CHOCOLATE AND BEETROOT BROWNIES

Makes about 12

85g dark chocolate, 75%
  cocoa solids

3 eggs

300g caster sugar

120ml sunflower oil

125g melted butter

300g cooked beetroot,
  peeled and puréed (shop
  bought is fine)

30g cocoa powder

200g plain flour

1½ tsp bicarbonate soda

LOVELY POLLY who has been very much part of this book gave me this recipe. I tried it and am now hooked. The combination of the juicy beetroot with the chocolate makes a really interesting brownie and so far they have been very popular.

I use a square baking tin for them and it works really well. Alternatively you can use a silicone cake mould. This needs no greasing at all but you will need to have it sitting on a baking sheet before filling!

—

Preheat oven to 180°C/gas mark 4. Line a 24cm x 24cm baking tin with greaseproof paper and lightly oil.

Melt the chocolate and butter in a heatproof bowl over a pan of simmering water. (This can be done VERY gently in a microwave but be careful as it does burn easily.)

In a large mixing bowl, lightly beat the eggs with the sugar and oil, gradually beat in the beetroot purée. Stir in the melted chocolate and butter. Sift the cocoa, flour and bicarbonate of soda over the surface and mix thoroughly.

Spoon the mixture into the tin or mould and bake for approximately 35 minutes or until light and springy. Leave to cool before cutting into squares.

Serve warm with the best vanilla ice cream you can get!

CHOCOLATE CAKE

Serves 8-10

175g self raising flour

150g caster sugar

2 tbsp cocoa powder

1 tsp bicarbonate soda

2 large eggs beaten

150ml sunflower oil

150ml semi skimmed milk

2 tbsp golden syrup

Topping:

 85g unsalted butter

175g icing sugar

3 tbsp cocoa powder

Drop of milk

This is truly delicious and perfect for any birthday occasion or party and straight forward too so make it and enjoy!

—

Pre-heat oven to 180°C/gas mark 4. Grease and line two 18cm sandwich tins.

Sieve the flour, cocoa and bicarbonate of soda into a bowl. Add the sugar and mix well.

Make a well in the centre and add the syrup, eggs, oil and milk. Beat well with electric whisk until smooth.

Spoon the mixture into the two tins and bake for 25-30 minutes until risen and firm to the touch. Remove from oven, leave to cool before turning out onto a cooling rack.

To make your butter icing, place the butter in a bowl and beat until soft. Gradually sift and beat in the icing sugar and cocoa powder then add enough milk to make the icing fluffy and spreadable.

If the cake has risen a little too high then use a serrated knife to even off the top, now sandwich the two cakes together with the butter icing and cover the top and/or the sides of the cake with more butter icing.

CLAUDIA RODEN'S MIDDLE EASTERN ORANGE AND ALMOND CAKE ⓖⒻ

2 oranges
5 eggs
250g ground almonds
225g sugar
1 tsp baking powder
Icing sugar, to serve

1 x 22cm spring form cake tin

THIS COMES FROM A BOOK BY CLAUDIA RODEN called 'A New Book of Middle Eastern Food'. I love it as it is gluten free and it also has no butter in which I think is brilliant. It makes a lovely pudding too with some greek yoghurt or vanilla ice cream.

———

Put the oranges in a large, deep saucepan, cover with water and bring to the boil. Simmer for about 1 hour or until very soft. Remove the oranges from the water and set aside to cool. Discard the water.

Preheat oven to 180°C/gas mark 4. Lightly grease the tin and line the base with baking powder.

Using a plate to catch the juices, cut the cooled oranges into quarters and remove the pips. Purée the quarters in a food processor or blender.

Beat the eggs in a large bowl until frothy, then beat in the orange puree. Fold in the almonds, sugar and baking powder and mix until combined. Pour the batter into the prepared tin and bake for 50-60 minutes, or until firm to the touch. Cook a little longer if needed.

Remove from the oven and cool in the tin for about 20 minutes before turning out onto a wire rack to cool completely. Dust with icing sugar to serve.

CRUNCHIE CHOCOLATE PEANUT BARS

Makes 20
250g salted peanuts
300g chocolate – 200g
  milk/100g plain
125g butter
4 Crunchie bars - crushed
3 tbsp syrup

A LOVELY CUSTOMER of ours Heather brought these delicious little treats into us one day – this is a Nigella recipe and they are simply gorgeous!

—

In a saucepan melt chocolate, butter and syrup together. Take off the heat and let it cool. Then add crunchies and peanuts. Stir well.

Pour into a 20cm square tin (silicone tins are good for this recipe).

Cool overnight and cut into squares.

CUPCAKES

Makes 12 muffin size cupcakes

250g Stork margarine

250g caster sugar

4 large eggs

250g self raising flour
 (if making chocolate change
 30g flour for cocoa powder)

Pinch of baking powder

1 tsp good quality vanilla
 essence

For the icing:

175g butter

350g icing sugar

2 tsp good quality vanilla
 essence

Dash of milk

THESE ARE MADE BY A LOCAL LADY and are to die for. Her decorations never fail to impress me, so be creative and try lots of different colours and decorations. Perfect for any age party; my Mum had them for her 60th.

———

Preheat the oven to 180°C/gas mark 4. Line a muffin tin with 12 cases.

Cream the margarine and sugar until pale and fluffy. Add the eggs gradually with a little of the flour, add the vanilla essence. Fold in the remainder of the flour and baking powder. Spoon in to the muffin cases and bake in a pre-heated oven at 180°C for 16 minutes.

Whilst the cakes are baking, make the icing. Cream the butter and icing sugar - add the vanilla essence to the milk before adding to the mixture.

Once removed from the oven, allow the cakes to cool, and then have fun decorating them however you wish.

FLAPJACKS

250g Stork margarine
250g demerara sugar
4 tbsp golden syrup
400g rolled oats

You can't beat a chewy but soft flapjack. Be careful not to overcook, they need to be a golden brown but still soft.

—

Preheat the oven to 160°C/gas mark 3. Lightly grease a 30 x 23cm roasting tin. (Line with baking parchment too - they will come out far easier).

Melt the margarine in a large pan with the sugar and syrup until the sugar has dissolved. Stir in the oats and mix well.

Turn into prepared tin and press down flat with a palette knife or back of a spoon.

Bake in the oven for approximately 35 minutes or until pale golden brown. Remove from the oven and leave to cool for 10 minutes.

Cut into slices before completely cool.

FRUIT SCONES

Makes 6-8 large scones
500g self raising flour
120g Stork margarine
Handful of sultanas
3 tbsp caster sugar
2 eggs beaten with
*   125ml milk*

A WINNING RECIPE - just try it. So many people say they can't make a good scone, I promise these work and are fab.

—

Preheat oven to 200°C/gas mark 6, and lightly grease a baking sheet or line with baking parchment.

Sift the flour into a mixing bowl. Add the margarine and mix to a fine crumb mixture, either with your fingers or a spatula works well.

Add the sugar and sultanas to the mixture and then carefully add the eggs with milk. You want to have a firm but light mixture. More flour can be added if it's too sticky.

Turn dough out onto a floured surface and pat the mixture down to the height of about 2cm. Using a 6cm cutter cut out the scones and put onto a baking tray.

Brush with a little beaten egg and bake for 15-20 minutes. Serve with homemade strawberry jam and clotted cream.

GINGER CAKE

300g soft margarine
400g golden syrup (half syrup
  and half treacle works well)
1 egg, beaten
130g plain flour
225g self raising flour
1 tsp ground ginger
1 tsp cinnamon
Pinch of salt
100g soft dark brown sugar
1½ tsp bicarbonate soda
1 tbsp finely chopped stem
  ginger

Preheat the oven to 150°C/gas mark 2. Grease and line a 26cm cake tin.

Melt the margarine and syrups in a pan. Place the flours, ginger, cinnamon, salt and sugar in a food mixer and mix at low speed.

Pour in the melted margarine and syrups and then add the egg. Dissolve the bicarbonate of soda in a cupful of water and then pour into the bowl with the mixer running.

Spoon into the prepared tin and bake for approximately 1 hour.

Leave to cool in the tin for 10 minutes before turning out onto a wire rack.

LEMON DRIZZLE CAKE

Makes 2 x 450g loaves
350g soft margarine
350g self raising flour
1 tsp baking powder
350g caster sugar
5 eggs
2 tbsp milk
Finely grated rind of 2 lemons

For the topping:
2 lemons, juice
100g sugar

MAKE 2 if you are making one, they are so good and you can always freeze one or give to a friend.

—

Preheat the oven to 180°C/gas mark 4. Grease and line 2 x 450g loaf tins or use a cake liner.

Measure all the cake ingredients into a large bowl and beat well for about 2 minutes. Place the mixture into the tins and level the surface of each.

Bake for about 30 minutes or until the cakes spring back when the surface is lightly pressed with the finger and have shrunk slightly from the sides of the tin.

Whilst the cakes are baking, make the crunchy topping. Mix lemon juice and sugar in a small bowl and stir to mix. Pierce the cake with a sharp knife or fork. Spread the lemon mix over the loaves whilst they are still hot and then leave to cool completely.

MOIST FRUIT CAKE

Makes 1 x 900g cake

125g butter

175g soft brown sugar

125g glace cherries, halved

375g dried mixed fruit

2 eggs

Small tin pineapple in juice, crushed

250g self raising flour

2 tsp mixed dried spice

A really good fruit cake that my lovely Mum makes, it doesn't stay around long as it's so delicious! Keep one in the tin for those unexpected friends or family coming by.

—

Preheat oven to 160°C/gas mark 3.

Grease a 900g loaf tin and line the base with baking parchment.

Place the butter, sugar, cherries and dried fruit into a large pan. Bring gently to the boil and simmer for 5 minutes. Allow to cool for 10 minutes.

Transfer the fruit mixture to a large mixing bowl. Add the beaten eggs and crushed pineapple. Sift the flour and mixed spice into the bowl and mix until well combined. Spoon the mixture into the prepared cake tin.

Bake for approximately 50-60 minutes, or until firm and a skewer inserted into the centre comes out clean. Leave to cool before turning out onto a wire rack.

SUGARLESS FRUIT CAKE

Makes 1 x 900g loaf

250g sultanas

250g dried apricots, chopped

200ml apple juice

150g soft margarine

250g self-raising flour

3 eggs, beaten

1 tsp bicarbonate of soda

THIS IS A DELICIOUS MOIST CAKE that is sugar free, so perfect for diabetics or anyone avoiding sugar.

—

Put the margarine on top of the fruit in a heatproof bowl and then pour over the apple juice.

Microwave for 10 minutes on a low power and then leave to soak for 6-8 hours or overnight.

The next day, preheat oven to 200°C/gas mark 6. Lightly grease a 900g loaf tin and line with baking parchment.

Mix the flour, eggs and bicarbonate of soda into the fruit mixture and then tip into loaf tin.

Bake in the oven for 50 minutes or until a skewer inserted into the middle comes out clean.

Party Time

FAMILY OR FRIENDS COMING TO VISIT? YOU WANT TO DO SOMETHING
WONDERFUL BUT CAN'T DECIDE WHAT TO PUT TOGETHER?
HERE'S A SELECTION OF WINNERS, ALL FROM ESTHER'S BEST.

QUICK MID-WEEK SUPPER
HOUMOUS, PITTA BREAD AND OLIVES 40
SMOKED HADDOCK, CHORIZO & CANNELLINI BEAN HOTPOT 50
GREEN SALAD
BERRY TRIFLE 85

—

SPECIAL DINNER FOR FRIENDS
TOMATO AND BASIL SOUP 18
PORK, APPLE, AND CIDER MEATBALLS WITH RICE 60
MUM'S DATE, HONEY AND WALNUT TART 95

—

A LIGHT LUNCH
MUSHROOM PÂTÉ WITH HOMEMADE WHITE BLOOMER 41, 25
PRAWN AND AVOCADO SALAD 33
MERINGUES WITH STRAWBERRIES AND CREAM 92

VEGETARIAN CELEBRATION MEAL

**OLIVE AND SUNBLUSHED TOMATO FOCACCIA
WITH CARAMELISED RED ONIONS** 23

**WARM BEETROOT, GOAT'S CHEESE AND
PUY LENTIL SALAD WITH LEMON AND HONEY DRESSING** 35

ROASTED VEGETABLE LASAGNE 77

LEMON MERINGUE PIE 91

—

A SUMMER BUFFET

ASPARAGUS TART 65

HERBY COUSCOUS WITH SPICY LAMB MEATBALLS 32, 62

ESTHER'S CRUNCHY COLESLAW 31

NEW POTATOES WITH MINT AND BUTTER

CHOCOLATE ROULADE 87

APRICOT AND VANILLA TART 84

CONVERSION CHARTS

At the Café we use metric weights and measures in our recipes, but if you prefer to use imperial or American cup measurements, then use these conversion charts.

Don't switch between metric and imperial in one recipe. There will be small discrepancies between equivalent weights and you could end up with the wrong proportions of ingredients.

Spoon measurements* convert easily to millilitres, and vice versa:
• 1 tablespoon is 15ml
• 1 dessertspoon is 10 ml
• 1 teaspoon is 5 ml

*Measuring spoons will correspond to this, although domestic cutlery may not.

Weight			
10g	¼oz	375g	13oz
15g	½oz	400g	14oz
25g	1oz	425g	15oz
50g	1¾oz	450g	1lb
75g	2¾oz	500g	1lb 2oz
100g	3½oz	700g	1½lb
150g	5½oz	750g	1lb 10oz
175g	6oz	1kg	2¼lb
200g	7oz	1.25kg	2 lb 12oz
225g	8oz	1.5kg	3 lb 5oz
250g	8oz	2kg	4½lb
275g	9¾oz	2.25kg	5lb
300g	10½oz	2.5kg	5½lb
350g	12oz	3kg	6½lb

Volume		
1.25ml	¼ tsp	
2.5ml	½ tsp	
5ml	1 tsp	
15ml	1 tbsp	
30ml	1 fl oz	
50ml	2 fl oz	
100ml	3½ fl oz	
150ml	5 fl oz	¼ pint
200ml	7 fl oz	
300ml	10 fl oz	½ pint
500ml	18 fl oz	
600ml	20 fl oz	1 pint
700ml		1¼ pints
850ml		1½ pints
1 litre		1¾ pints
1.2 litres		2 pints

Oven temperatures			
Celsius	Fahrenheit	Gas Mark	Description
110°C	225°F	¼	cool
130°C	250°F	½	cool
140°C	275°F	1	very low
150°C	300°F	2	very low
170°C	325°F	3	low
180°C	350°F	4	moderate
190°C	375°F	5	moderate/hot
200°C	400°F	6	hot
220°C	425°F	7	hot
230°C	455°F	8	very hot

For fan-assisted ovens reduce temperature by 20°C.

American measurements All weights below = 1 cup (unless specified)			
Butter, Margarine, Lard		Dried Pulses	
110g 8tbsp = 1 stick		Lentils	225g
	225g = 1 cup	Haricot beans	200g
Breadcrumbs		Kidney beans	185g
Fresh	50g	Rice	
Dried	125g	Uncooked	200g
Cheese		Cooked & drained	135g
Grated cheddar	115g	Sugar	
Grated parmesan	100g	Caster	200g
Cream cheese	225g	Granulated	200g
Dried fruit		Icing sugar	140g
Sultanas	175g	Vegetables	
Apricots	150 -175g	Onions, chopped	125g
Prunes	180-200g	Potatoes, peeled	150g
Flour	140g	Tomatoes	175g
Golden syrup, treacle,		Fish	
clear honey	350g	Prawns, peeled	190g
Liquids	225ml	Cooked, flaked	225g
Nuts		Meat	
Almonds, whole	135g	Minced	225g
Almonds, flaked	100g		
Walnuts & pecans	115g		
Oats			
Rolled oats	100g		
Oatmeal	140g		

Weights and volumes are in line with the Guild of Food Writers' guidelines

ESTHER'S BEST RECIPE BOOK has only been possible because of the ideas, encouragement, recipes, contributions and support from the following people; very big thank yous to: Ursula Ferrigno for suggesting the idea and her positive support. Julia Harvey for so much foodie help over the years. Polly Royle, Alice, Em and Oliver for tasting recipes painfully. Ros Plummer for food styling. Lucy Johnston and assistant Freya Richmond for the photos. Sally Burch for an enormous contribution to the Café and her brilliant website design. My mum for her generosity, cakes and for always being there. Zara my sister, for her inspiration and enthusiasm. Auntie Anne for encouragement and support along the way. Kath Lees for her amazing artistic talent and for getting a vision for the book so quickly and easily. The staff at Mistley Quay, with a special mention to Debbie who has worked with me to create a lot of the recipes, Karen, Tash and all the girls. Lovely Jackie who has made life smooth and happy and looked after my 2 children so well. Local friends and customers without whom none of it would be possible. Most of all my faithful and wonderful husband Richard, and children, Freddie and Eliza.

Esther

ESTHER'S BEST SUPPLIERS

GETTING your produce from the right place is so important. I always think that if you have good quality ingredients and keep things simple you can't go wrong. What could be better than fine cheese, organic leaves and fresh bread made from organic flour?

Alison's Organics
Alison supplies wonderful salad leaves, eggs and seasonal produce. Available from the Wholefood Store.

Coleman's Butchers
Excellent local meats
01206 272270

The Company Shed
Famous local restaurant and supplier of oysters, fish and seafood.
01206 382700

Fresh Produce Wholesale
Fresh local fruit and veg
01787 460772

Freshpac Teas & Coffees
Suppliers of very good coffee
01986 873410

Hadley's Ice Cream
Homemade and very tasty, made locally, all by hand!
01787 220420

Hamish Johnston
Suffolk based cheese supplier (also in London)
01728 621544

Nethergate Wines
All our wines are supplied by this excellent wine merchant
01284 852110

Scoffers
A local bakery that supplies tasty bread and florentines
01206 393118

Sladbury's Farm Smokehouse
Local, traditionally 'home smoked' salmon
01255 812042

Wholefood Store
Wonderful local shop; fresh produce, dried grains and pulses, dried fruit, spices and exotic ingredients
01206 391200

INDEX

INDEX

(GF) Any recipe marked with
this symbol is gluten free

INDEX

**ESTHER'S BEST
STORE CUPBOARD ESSENTIALS:**
CHILLIES
CRUSHED BLACK PEPPER
GARLIC
GOOD QUALITY OLIVE OIL
GOOD QUALITY TINNED CHOPPED TOMATOES
MALDON SALT
MARIGOLD VEGETABLE STOCK (GLUTEN FREE)
MIXED DRIED HERBS
PUMPKIN & SUNFLOWER SEEDS
RED & PUY LENTILS
TOMATO PURÉE
VANILLA EXTRACT
WHITE WINE VINEGAR

SIMPLY PERFECT RECIPES
Esther's Best
RECIPE BOOK
WITH ZEST. ENGLAND